Jiggers

Jiggers

Todd Bruce

Turnstone Press

Turnstone Press
607 – 100 Arthur Street
Winnipeg, Manitoba
Canada R3B 1H3

Turnstone Press gratefully acknowledges the assistance of the Canada Council and the Manitoba Arts Council.

A short and somewhat altered selection from *Jiggers* appeared in *Prairie Fire,* Vol. 12, No. 1 (Spring 1991)

Cover photograph from the Five Days of Suspicion (detail)
Laurence Peter Mardon © 1993

Text design: Manuela Dias

This book was printed and bound in Canada by Kromar Printing for Turnstone Press.

Canadian Cataloguing in Publication Data

Bruce, Todd, 1965–

Jiggers
Poems.
ISBN 0-88801-175-X

I. Title.

PS8533.R8J5 1993 C811'.54 C94-920007-7
PR9199.3.B78J5 1993

once again, for you

Jiggers might not have been written without the encouragement of Dennis Cooley (and his bag full of rhymes), the careful eye of Lorna Crozier, or the questions of Robert Kroetsch: to them I offer my thanks, my respect. And to Rob, who listened through wires, holes in the wall, blankets of smoke, to the construction of it all.

Contents

Jiggers

osmosis

there are places

we may land

in hard

metal

places

trees are copper

&

in fall

you hear

nothing but

leaves

chinking on

the zinc

sidewalks

they break

down

el a men tul par tik uls

soak in

to iron

gardens gold grass

mercury puddles blobbing through sewer grates

you : : : : : : : : : : are the only organic

alloy

alive lips

puFFed

out

like

a carp

sediments metallically under

your tongue

in 1 2 fil 3 4 tra 5 6 ting 7 8

counting is subconcious don't you

know

your body

the resistance yet

to be built

your tin collar clamped vice-like against your ears

helmet strapped tight around your chin

metal net mittens tied through your sleeves

the cord cutting your neck

you

try

not

to breathe try not to

breathe try not to

Times & Places

*

neither surprised nor horrified
when you told me
Jiggers died
yesterday in the Balmoral
in the Balmoral rooms are cheap
and so's the booze
nor was I saddened there'd been
no mass no
hullabaloo you said
you forgot him
it was easy

remember thinking
the dead are exempt

neither surprised nor horrified
I wasn't I
told you not to worry about it I'd
take care of everything
go ahead with your vacation I

told you not to worry about it I'd
bury him tomorrow somewhere
you couldn't find him I

listened to the drone
of silence that tripped in after
the connection broke

Jesus stinks

in the Balmoral Hotel
hangs there in
splatters of beer & baby
duck water
logged Christ
bowing low
chin to chest some
where to the left
is Jiggers bed

I used to be a silent man
hands of a potter
Mary dripped away
I could sing

deli sandwich
spit in his beard
tired rotten eyes wet
brain dissolving his eye
searches me for the bottle

I used to be a silent man
hands of a potter
I could sing

Jiggers liked to drink
with an amateur careful
not to spill until
he stumbles to his
feet gently bathes
the drifting son
of man genuflects his
chin to his chest

I used to be a silent man
I could sing

*

there is a long catalogue
so many things to remember
one of them being Jiggers

singing inside
Blessed Sacrament Church
black silk pants
towering over
stilted legs his
head lifted into the stained
glass balcony his
left hand grasping
the piano edge
so the notes
won't stray he
says you know
how notes can run off
being notes and all

his voice becoming
yours loud clear
notes (ring) floating
into the musty air clinging
to the wood beams scattered
by the ceiling
fans

when you walk away
from the sanctuary you
look back
quickly
afraid your
eye surveys the steeple
for musty escapees
on of them being Jiggers

Defenestration

The taxi driver is shrouded in a dingy halo thrown through
the cracks and scratches of the shield   between us.
He is smoking his fist, a crumpled,   handrolled cigarette,
his eyes glinting like rusted steel in   the rear view mirror.
We cannot speak. I cannot tell   him anything but a street
name, a number, an address.   My eyes combat the fog
in the foreground and find   their way outside where
everything flows by with   the whipping trail of cigarette
smoke. A siren splices   the winter streets. It cuts and
drops away in the fine slit   of a wake. And I did not
know where I was when   I screamed for him to let me
out. Just found a pub   that was willing to let me become
its background, a   bar that was willing to let me cut &
drop, in its lap, a halo

sun sprocket
(for ellen)

Jiggers built a bi
cycle at night
in his garage
metals and fire

back wheel blurred
scintillation of rods
spokes molded by hand
straightened in concrete jackets
cracked apart like sunflower seeds
threaded & cut & poked
arcing & springing & vibrating
soundful into the rim

hot beads like sweat
silver marbles solder
wrapping like a sponge
clamping a hiss
a cobalt hand a
solid prayer

ground a gear from the shop to size
whittled it with fire
painted it chrome
polished in a shirt sleeve
a silver mirror
shiny mini moon
sun sprocket orbit axis

a tin-snipped baby
blue pin
striped chain
guard

Jiggers consoles the sun the moon
wet silent sagging chain
wraps it and sprinkles it with oil
pops rivets removes links
a tender perfection of tense
linking xoanons
a natural harmony
whisper of marriage
breath of music
clanging crisp and bright
a fist clenched to strike a bell

the frame burst from the hands
a craftsman a
potters wheel a
sculptors stool

—hollow holey pipes
hum & whir & whistle in wind
wild flutes & piccolos & saxophones &
Jiggers could make it sing
Jesus could he ever
he pedaled songs
moving the sun like a sprocket
the moon like a gear

CN

a banging bell or a
clanging symbol a
jangling Jiggers
arc welder
metal pounder
rock cracker
chain locker

Out side
bi
cycles
four foot square
cinder blocks cubes
clamped together
mossy lined (a
struck *churr* a
black iron plate a
bell fat walls a
humming) a
whistling Jiggers
ring-eyes goggling
rubber hands &
puppet arms

fire spilling
sparks white a
star sharp
in a CN night in a
CN day in a three
o clock clamping
a lid

spring-eyed men
tongues sniffling the wind
tarnished silver-eyed men

Jiggers jangling a
lone be
hind spin
ning a top
smoke puffs
from his hair a

whiskey to loosen
the joints a
whiskey to screw
shut the mind

There are dangers in watching a man drown

his finger bones
showing through skin
bare from clutching
the rocks there are
dangers in pouring change
into a beggars hands you
look him inthe eye & he is
shiny-faced from your past &
singing pockets full of change

when he hangs on
long as he can legs up
to the thigh heavy
with tide
you sense him
beginning to slip
away you hear bones
scrape across
the rocks you

the skies do not
open you crouch in front arms
extended a hostile tear the tide you
say nothing arms &
for months you wake

<table>
<tr><td>him there</td><td>fresh as a paper cut</td><td>his bloodied hands</td></tr>
<tr><td>the rip</td><td>the scrape</td><td>the jag in the rock</td></tr>
<tr><td>his face</td><td>ugly and creased</td><td>fear &</td></tr>
<tr><td>his eyes</td><td>paling</td><td>into yours</td></tr>
</table>

Places & Times

Mary's boy

do you remember
Junior died
a suicide

slit his ankles
five inches deep
started walking
home to you
heels clicking
like thongs

his sound before pain

the trail
of tendons he left
you as
he collapsed
eaten by ravens

after church

at Jiggers house
where Mary lives &
margarine melts
hot biscuits

how she hugs me &
laughs at the tie
round my neck

how she hugs me &
undresses me
peels the starch
the skin from my body

how she leads me up
stairs cool hand on my back

how she dresses me
in play clothes
(sits on the porch)
with tea and oranges

how she whispers to me
the secret lives of plants
wild licorice pokeweed pale comandra

how she tells my parents
nothing when they seize me
shiny-faced and spotless & take me
home for catechism

widow

the anger from your eyes

him face down on the road
his ankles slit
tendons ripped
and loose blood

steps zagging behind
his ankles
clacked like untied sandals

we buried him
in the river with blessings
you tasted his blood
let him go

you made love that night
to me curling your long arms
and legs like webs
around me your face
you shivered and cried
and then let go
the taste of blood
warm beneath your lips

I watched you sleeping and I
dreamed for you
I opened the window and I
watched the night for you
the night we became lovers
the night I became your son

watched you slip
through the window

the silver outside
the raven who flees
like night mixed in
your long black hair

Hymn
(for Charlene)

I

you call me
full of words

your mouth is not attached
to your body we are
naked in a blue & pewter
bright as the sky
wherein your heart is
laid the softness of your speech
upon my shoulder linger
my skin

you call me
full of words

sepe
nipeya
nemehtow

I will
not swim
cannot surface

a fool caught in a river
a ghost in a tree
shivering on the night air
my white bird bones

call me *sepe*
I will rattle and spin
inside this river's jam

call me *nipeya*
I will speak you sanctuary

call me *nemehtow*
and I shall dance the dance
for you

I&I

when I was born
you searched into my eye
you looked for a ring of orange
and you lifted me
into the sky
your neck arched back
long hair sweeping
the earth like planets
toward the moon
falling from your shoulders
onto sand

do you remember
washing me in the river
the cold stare
eyes in the
night everywhere

I am
here again mother blood
everything I
touch I touch
unenveloping you
the river
lapping I
cannot feel

and then
the sky turns

I&I&I

        when you do
not come to me
I feel you
the most when I
build the blank
sky a fortress of purple
& yellow
frame for you the sky
and you will
not come to meI
feel you the most

        when I
search for you
breathlessly under
the river when I
fear to prepare
to surface and you
place a bubble
about my skull I
feel you least

when it is cold
and I am tired
when I am sure
you are lost

The Other Than

Princess

Jiggers and Mary were lovers.

Jiggers watched
a peering eye
a window dusty with frost
a favorite table in The Princess Hotel

The Princess, whiskeys dropped
warm & ringng

Jiggers' hands a
sculptor's hands

—snow like saw
dust blowing
past town—

supple & strong a
closed hand
turning

slowly the snow
drifts in dunes
across the tracks across
Pandora Avenue lit
in blinking neon a
perfect darkness (no)
moonlight just unlight

—something in a black
sea the perfect hiding—

eyes in the night

"Cold one." (Bob squeaks a beer
glass dry. Bob lies
tells stories a little
advice.) "Not going no wheres ta nite."

snow banks curl in
to question marks

—the undertow—

                    a black period

the end of town

Mary

handmaiden to the night
footsteps move to darkness
framed in neon black
half in
the light
moon slipping a
veil over an eye
Jiggers whiskey in the window
the lights dimming
in the Princess

—freight train crashing through drifts
yellow eyes through the box car slats
snouts scrambling for a taste of air
cold as frozen milk—

Jiggers waiting
boot tongues
rumbling of a train
the smell of cow shit
passing through him
the sweat in his hair
cooled into ice

the floating eye of a caboose

[& open]

darkness the ink

[blot]

night stretching around in
wide-eyed death

the compact snow
giving way
they leave prints in snow
the sound of Mary   howling

Taken

sizzling crystals
snow ice
hardened to shards of sun
flaring like fire
the focused eye of a torch

a full page of white

a scuffle of
prints a
frozen patch
blood stiffens on

a clearing asylum as snow
angels a zagging

track of frozen clothes

—silence
a switching off—

face directly into the wind
and you may not hear it

A

when Jiggers sings an
A the guitar
hums from its stand &
the piano vibrates like
A vocal chord &
the saxophone whistles
A hollow whistle

when Jiggers sings an
A instruments surrounding him
like friends when Jiggers sings an
A there is
A natural harm
on
E

From the Eye

a tear or
a tear

Jig

Jig

Jiggers in the park
joggers jogging
getting high

brains like cold porridge
like petrified mush
rooms everywhere
grey brains on lawns
kids throwing them
like footballs
tripping over them

footfalls on a
cool October sun
see across a river through the trees day
see the cone head
the legislature now
a nakedness
a cool muddy swim away

Jiggers on a swing
in a sandbox
brand new bottle
tequila, what he drinks
when he drinks
in the park

this is when the woman comes

woman in black
coat red scarf
coming close her clatter
on the circular pavement

she drops a newspaper on a brain
bows politely-like
to Jiggers &
loosens her arms into the fifth
position pulls up
her spine dangles
from a string anchors
in a cloud

this is what her feet say

(read it out loud)

fullap fullap fullap ball change
leap shuffle touch ball change
leap shuffle touch ball change
bom bro shay
bom bro shay
bom bro shay
dig!

hop

toe

hop

leap

hop

toe

hop

shuf

fle

hop

step

shuf

fle

heel

step

brush

heel

step brush heel step

brush heel

toe

she tap dances for him
just like that
her vaudeville feet say

then she crawls like a spider
up the string &
vanishes into a cloud
all that and never breaking fifth
position it was amazing
you would have been amazed

this is what happens
after the woman
disappears into the cloud

Jiggers teeters on a see-saw
ass sagging over the wooden plank
watches the cloud drift away

4/4

i cannot tap

dance for you you

watch my feet too

much you do not

listen to the

rhythm i can

dance the beat

your heart says you'd

never know you

do not listen

to the rhythm

choreography

i want you
on a lamplit sidewalk
in a quiet park
past midnight
in an overcoat
a sagging breast
pocket a bottle of scotch
i want you
to walk in a rhythm
like this

& a 1
& a 2
& a 3 a
& a 4

i want you
to raise your hands
next to the left
side of your face
i want you
to clap
in double time

1 & 2
3 & 4
1 & 2 3
& 4

i will be falling
off the park bench
falling in love

Jiggers had a friend
named Alice after Mary and Junior
died.

bettern hot soup

the night that Mary died
cold & brilliant
sky glowing black
starry starry
northern lights like mad dogs
running in broken harnesses
the night that Mary died
three years after her son
three years six
hours & twelve minutes
after the death of her son

the night I followed him carefully
Jiggers met Alice
under the Osborne
bridge across from the legislature
below the high-rises
beside the Assiniboine
next to a fire
fueled by newsprint
                                                he sat

her lone crumpled figure painted with fire
a bottle she pushes it through the fire toward him
the loose stitches of her coat
frizzling so close to the fire
go ahead she says
s bettern hot soup

the night that Mary died
cold & brilliant
sky glowing black
starry starry
north

i waited until the sun came
to a boil
until Sal perfumed the glassy air
& diesels crawled sleepily over uncertain ice
& sparrows zagged across the muddy river waves

until below my perch their bodies moved and stretched
& hunger roused them into the eye
dirt of the blinking city

until they walked below me
arm in arm singing a song

until the river stopped breathing
puffs of smoke

i waited until the sky percolated in its opaque carafe
me a sieve
a silex pouring through

scotch on a Sunday

she says
you must be rich

bare feet over the cool wood
floor her fingers
            bruised
a dieffenbachia

used to keep plants
                     she says
a garden too and
a son lot like you
says she loves weddings

bottle sweating in
front of her
handed me a polished war
medal she holds
the case says
a ring came in it says
she wanted to keep it
alive loved the sound

when I bring out the photo album
she hardly believes it's him
I quickly flip the page before
she can point her
long index finger at Mary

Alice gone
quickly as the scotch
her mesh bag
crumpling on the floor
waving by the fan
where her soft feet
once cooled

Tricks

Tricks

sure Jiggers was an alcoholic
but he had rules
only drank alone
less he was broke
& wouldn't drink in a bar
unless the barkeep's name was Bob

oh you think that's strange eh
hunh bet you got some tricks
of your own

youve got a trick
up your s
                    leave

Bob tells stories

he was fixing the sink
under the bar
shouting to us
cross the way
clanking this and muttering that

"Met this girl once. Hell, must of been no more than seventeen at the time. Don't know about her though. Maybe the same, maybe a year older. She was a painter that one, a real artiste, not houses you know, real pictures like in the museum."

Jiggers in the 4 o clock dusk
legs in spasms
eye focused somewhere on the wall
steel toed boots kick me under the table
nose twitching
his hands are lost to his control
strings were attached
everyone pulling

"Hell, can't imagine what Christly thing got into us that night. Went ice skating out on Horse Pond. Had a bottle of the old man's apple wine. Froze like gangbusters though, quicker than milk. But jumping Jesus could that woman skate. Double jumps, spins, all sorts a that fancy stuff."

Jiggers wearing down
a battery of things
that are silent
five one ounce shots of whiskey
look up at him and wait
a ring of calibrated glasses
a glass eye
when his hands stop shaking
he will pour them like oil
into his throat

"Cracked the bottle open on the rink and chopped the wine into ice cubes. Sucked on them like grapes. (The ringing of a hammer on stainless steel.) Godamit to hell anyway! These pipes won't budge an inch."

mixed metaphors

never mixed his drinks
that Jiggers
straight whiskey straight
wine straight beer

never missed a trick neither
hung over like hell
but always prepared
big jug of water
for the thirsties
in the fridge
a little scotch for colour

used to dream
that Jiggers—

metal water fountains
and dew-soaked apple trees
blue icebergs and cool marshes
straws that reached from the kitchen to his bed

dreamt freshly squeezed orange
juice and seven-up
orchards stuffed with whiskey trees
always ripe

kept his Lowry
next to his bed

never mixed his drinks though
that Jiggers
cept maybe for a little
scotch in the thirsties jug

every good boy

got old Jiggers stoned once
trying to get him off the booze you know

sucked on that joint like it was candy
told me I couldn't roll worth hell
says watch out or I'll get busted
says so what the hell's supposed to happen now
not gonna see the devil am I

Jiggers says gimme the rest of that stuff
I'll roll em up decent for ya
hands like a magician that Jiggers
rolled em with filters ripped from a match box
no bulges even just even and narrow he even
clamped the lighting end tight so none would fall out

says Jesus this stuff is weird
unplugs the phone, locks the door
sits quiet as a parcel and whispers to me

I could sing ya know
wanna hear me sing

picks up his old El Dégas
three string guitar
all he ever had
not a trick neither
prefers it that way
Bob would buy him strings
2 Es
2 Gs
2 Bs

played em like magic too
like a harp or something
never watched the pattern
couldn't follow it even
just listened to it
cruise like music can cruise

a blues shuffle slow and tender
slow and tense
and he'd sing Amazing Grace
in G to the blues

ahhhhhhhha may zieeing grace
how oow see ee eet the e sound

Early winter
a diary

10/15/89
6:04 am

remember that really cold weather
remember how mom use to dress you
mitts tucked into your sleeves
scarf wrapped like a head bandage
and long johns and dad's work socks
and a hooded sweater and a parka
that covered your pecker tied with a belt
and ski pants that smooshed when you walked
your hood tied so tight
you couldn't see a thing
and the grade sixers use to say
you looked like a blue daisy
blooming in the snow and
push you over
                                        remember how
you'd lie in the hot snowbank
lake a ladybug on her back

well that's how cold it was
when you phoned to say
you miss me

you knew I wouldn't come

10/15/89
6:21 am

When the air is crunchy with chill. When you have to hike up your shorts to warm your nuts. When you squeeze shut your legs and a shiver slips out like a fart. When you scrunch your nose and feel the frost ripping apart your nostril hairs. When you begin to wish for two hot cups of tea nestled against your ears (like muffs) and your last concern is a cold beer. When you know like you can know that they will have to cut off your toes. When sounds are clingering in the air and you cannot touch them. When you know to stop trying. It is at that moment you begin to scratch the surface. It is then you begin to understand.

10/21/89
11:14 pm

Sleep, I have to sleep.

10/22/89
6:42 am

all packed
waiting for fire
to die

knees feel like kindling

it hurts

fox tracks
for a while
then nothing

eagle hasn't left
wonder why

hope the car starts

10/10/89
5:49 am

beautiful sunrise today
nothing like twenty years ago

snow is spilled
around poplar trunks
in white molasses

quiet here

owl pretending to sleep
in the Jack

knees aching today
never ache like this before

lake acting like its frozen
played that game before

nothing like the sun
beaming at you
its face on the other side
a thick pane of ice

head home soon

kettle boiling

11/11/90
noon?

cold wind like snow
stove eating wood like
a stove eating wood

a dead pelican this morning
frozen in the lake
its webbed feet frozen
it tried to leave
something got at it
just below the neck
wolf I guess
scared away though
wonder why

1/27/90
1:20 am

low, fast moving cloud
smoke on a navy night
the moon like a beam
a miner's lamp
the stars, distant in the shaft

I listen, she says, to everything
you say through a screen

people below him, the street
in the snow
walk quickly
their hands pushed into pockets
it takes three seconds
for them to enter and to leave
the frame   his window pane

I can't, he says, afford that

Intraveneous

too many words   at war to become one thought   the fear
of speaking is bound in experience   that one time you gave
them five thoughts and they picked one and chose it as your best
    the language   the words   the people   in them all
    demanding meaning   names   explanations

                                        bagpipes
    scotch   beside me   the car   touching my thigh
    nothing on the radio yet the radio   its sense of evaporation
on the highway yet it is November   for a moment   three
miles

        I curse myself for insisting a history into it   my relatives
      even the ones buried here feared this country   yet   I am
half drunk and squeezing the air with my elbow   feeling the
notes   round and fat   watching them float across the
cemetary like soap bubbles   collapsing somewhere in
Steinbach   it happens   I am as amazingly Scottish as the
grace that slips and floats in the fat notes

                                    the scent of freshly
turned mud   you never forget   the grass pokes its way
through your socks   cold stings   you note the absence of
mourning in the city worker's face   sipping from a thermos
in his bright yellow truck   and then of course   you
are reminded that nothing is rehearsed   you are not
sure which would be best   more scotch or hot
coffee   but of course you have no hot coffee

he
stands on the only rise he can find   lets the wind move his hair
relishes in its not being anything but air   this game
wishes a movie camera were somewhere in the distance
a record of false movements   he wants
someone to cry   wants someone to rise from the
dead   his widow to come with a wicker basket full of
poppies   or wild flowers she grew in her rock garden   he
wants her to be dressed in black   he wants her to walk with a
slouch

he wants to catch words   pin them on Styrofoam

he inserts the empty bottle of scotch
upside down into the belly of the grave and he loves how
giving the earth still is

*

yeah, ol Jiggers had a bird
or two
in the hand
may/be a dozen of em
orange ones
yellow ones
green ones
blue birds
purple too
all hanging
in cages
on his balcony
in the summer
flapping like
noisy flags
over main
higgins
squawking and
singing
one day
early in spring
when he was drunk
Jiggers let them go

*

My parrot flew straight into the electric heater. Got tangled in the coils. Fried to death. It was untimely. I was sad. He was purple. Had orange spots on his cheeks. This was before the heater. Quite surreal, everything about him, even his death.

My wife hated birds. Even little ones. Thought they would peck out her eyes. She had a thyroid condition. She never liked me much either. There was a lot about me she didn't care for. She left. She had yellow hair. Had brown eyes, pale skin. Quite beautiful, everything about her, even her absence.

She knows about my purple bird. Haven't told her that he is dead. I keep up my guard

Generally, people are afraid of birds. Cages, cheap metaphors, wings. The incarceration of symbols, the reservation of freedom. Birds with olive branches, talons. Birds of prey. They like that; people. Silent attacks. Ravens and crows. Lists. Parallels: people are afraid of parallels. Afraid to spell incorrectly.

I was sad. My parrot was dead. The smell, my god, it stunk, the smell of burnt feathers. The squawk! It was terrible. Almost plucked a tail feather but thought it might hurt. Was dead for three days before I could bring myself to touch him. I was hoping for a resurrection, parrot rising out of the ashes. I chose though, after some consideration, not to mythologize him.

Descant: The Final Entry

*

been pickin some tomatoes
from a sweet sweep of sun
(((Dawn

spreadin out my arms
ribbons from my tongue

can dance!
cadence
(the fall
the voice)

rushes through

kiss the honey tongue

kiss the honey tongue
perhaps my feet are wet with dew
morning shepherded into my heart

flowers announce themselves
cocking their heads
forgetting my name
written on their petals
a bee
makes love

to their eyes

or a code comes a cross
the tops of some trees
& moon (swollen cheek) quickly blinks

blood-shot eye
throws her hair in a net
tea bagging me
& dipped
am I bobbing
sucked under
& released
bobbing
I bob
and rain
shakes on me
wedded to your mouth
strings

✶

or else I want to be back in your living room (big glass of wine)
with your antique piano
the rocking chair you bought for twenty-five bucks
(want to make a hole in the clouds and look at you)
hear your fingers tap tap tap
stare into the window at night
while you ask yourself, down the hall, if there are mirrors
in heaven or books

to run my bare feet across your cold hardwood floors
pass my hand through the space where once was a wall
and remember you with a hammer smashing through it
tears on your face, letting sunlight in,
the dogs padding nervously down the hall

Ruby Mist

sip
or to tea
under a canopy of ash
after the harvest
in twilight

seeing (you through) hazes

Still Life with Turkey Pie

"We find courage not with
but rather in
the tips of our fingers."

You were pretending to be
in Amsterdam, but I
know the post card
came from Victoria.
Still
your words
have punctuated my life.

What does it mean to say *still life?*

"Still Life"

Stasis, freeze frame, whip in hand, signature.

But I must tell you,

I was described as "shocking" the other day. Of course, this came as a complete surprise to me when in fact my life is a response to how shocked I am, at every moment, by the status quo.

Still Life:
how impossible it seems,
these words, next to
one another. But then
again, I have a problem
with language.

Still,
I use it.
You can tell,
of course,
I am weary, tired after all.
Tough place to be, here is.

Surprised all together
the post card
even arrived.

Makes you wonder.

Dream of ever kissing you,
the filling of your mind,
photographing you
as you come,
still life.

courage: heart as the seat of

cor: heart

& courage for what
when in fact
I have plucked my heart
from my breast
and lay it at your feet
a small poem meant to be sung
a wager and a stake

an unfolding of ink
is all

a listening
an echo

a remembering
to forget

an invitation
to tea and biscuits

to a tolling of bells

to taste my breath

to touch my body